TABLE OF CONTE

The Publishing Agreement
What Every Author Should Know About Publishing Contracts
©Copyright 2013 by Dr. Leland Benton with Contributing Author
Kathy Hensel Porter

DISCLAIMER AND TERMS OF USE AGREEMENT:

(Please Read This Before Using This Book)

This information is for educational and informational purposes only. The content is not intended to be a substitute for any professional advice, diagnosis, or treatment.

The author and publisher of this book and the accompanying materials have used their best efforts in preparing this book.

The author and publisher make no representation or warranties with respect to the accuracy, applicability, fitness, or completeness of the contents of this book. The information contained in this book is strictly for educational purposes. Therefore, if you wish to apply ideas contained in this book, you are taking full responsibility for your actions.

The author and publisher disclaim any warranties (express or implied), merchantability, or fitness for any particular purpose. The author and publisher shall in no event be held liable to any party for any direct, indirect, punitive, special, incidental or other consequential damages arising directly or indirectly from any use of this material, which is provided "as is", and without warranties. As always, the advice of a competent legal, tax, accounting, medical or other professional should be sought where applicable.

Introduction – The Publishing Agreement from both Sides of the Equation

As Editor-in-Chief of ePubWealth, a full service international publishing house with over 1,000 authors under contract and with more than 40,000 books in inventory, I deal with Publishing Agreements on a daily basis and the first thing I want to teach you is that no two agreements are the same.

As Editor-in-Chief of ePubWealth, I will teach you what publishers want in the agreement. As the author of over 200-books on Amazon alone, I am able to also teach you what every author should have in the publishing agreement. You will be getting the best of both worlds.

In the olden days (and still somewhat true today), we dealt exclusively with the author's literary agent in negotiating publishing agreements. The book publishing industry is changing rapidly and author's literary agents are no longer as important as they once were.

This book only applies to authors that are seeking publishing houses to publish their content. This book DOES NOT apply to self-publishing indie authors, who act as their own publisher.

Back in 1980, when I began writing books, I was thrilled when a major New York publishing house contracted with me to publish my first novel and three other sequel novels too. At the time, I had visions of sugar plums dancing in my head as I reached out to my goal of becoming a best-selling author.

Well, feed me garlic and call me stinky, my experience with the New York publishing house was sheer disaster. They not only did a poor job of marketing my book, but I quickly realized that if my book did not garner a good amount of sales on the first promotion, I was placed in the back of the line as a bench-sitting author.

Now one thing you should know about me; I am not a milquetoast kind of guy. I raised holy hell with my agent and publisher contact and succeeded in being heard and getting action. Yep, they fired me and when I went to pour over my agreement with them I soon learned that the agreement was completely written in their favor with me as the second-class citizen.

Before you begin to feel sorry for me…DON'T…it is because of this little episode that I formed my own publishing house – ePubWealth – and never looked back.

It took me just a little over three years to reach best-selling author status and learn the ropes of the publishing business and because of the dynamics of publishing; it is always a continuing work-in-progress. With the advent of the Internet, promotion and marketing has become an art form and as one of my most famous sayings indicates, "Nothing happens until you sell something."

Almost daily, I come across good authors with multiple books in their inventory but nothing published. Amazing! I sincerely hope you are not one of these authors.

Authors are special people; without authors the world would be ignorant. We make our readers feel, we make them think; we entertain, cajole and speak from the heart.

In 2007 Amazon introduced the Kindle eReader – the first version sucked canal water so Amazon went back and redesigned it. In the mean time other companies began introducing their own eReaders –

Sony eReader, Barnes and Noble Nook, and more…in fact too many to list.

I was skeptical at first that the eReader devices would catch on and Amazon's marketing muscle did a full court press in promotion to get it to succeed. EReaders didn't catch on at first but history proves they are now a raging success.

The latest version of the Kindle eReader is the Kindle Fire HD, which isn't a bad unit but will probably be the last Kindle produced. EReaders are on their way out and the tablet is replacing them.

The tablet costs just about as much as an eReader device but a tablet is a full-service computer where most eReaders are not. With all of eReader apps available to turn your laptop into an eReader, tablets are certain to kill all eReader sales and they are doing it now.

Okay, let's move on. In my book, "How To Write Compelling Content", I demonstrate the behavioral science behind the written word. I have been a behavioral scientist for some 32-years now and this book is a very different kind of book and one you should read.

http://www.amazon.com/dp/B00B5QWYTI

This book is part of my ePublishing series of books. Because you bought this book, write to me: lee.benton@epubwealth.com and select one of the books below and I will send you the Adobe Acrobat PDF version of the book as my gift to you.

Okay, time's a wasting so let's get at it…

Chapter 1 – The Need for Publishing Agreements & Checklist

The need for publishing agreements has never been greater than in today's publishing marketplace. The industry is so dynamic and is changing almost daily. In order to keep up, both publishing houses and authors have a need to protect themselves. And the operative word here is "protect".

As an author, if a publisher tells you that you don't need an agreement run...don't walk....run away as fast as you can!!! Publishing agreements are standard operating procedures in the publishing industry. Yes, they can be tedious and in most cases authors would do well to hire competent legal counsel to make sure the author knows everything contained in the agreement and is satisfied with its contents.

I have placed a whole bunch of resources in a download portal (see the list below). Go here to retrieve them:

http://tinyurl.com/aze36w8

- Sample Publishing Contract – this is a short to the point agreement.

- SAMPLE PUBLISHING AGREEMENT2 - this is the one I use as a starting point and th\en I modify it in negotiations.
- PublishingAgreementv12w_dymmocks – I included this to show you a variety of publishing agreement available.
- Author-series_monograph_license – this is a standard agreement where the author retains ownership and copyright.
- HOW TO READ A PUBLISHING AGREEMENT – I included this as an instructional guide on the pertinent points an author needs to consider.
- TERMINATING A PUBLISHING AGREEMENT – Yes, you can terminate a publishing agreement but be careful to do it within the agreement's guidelines so you do not set yourself up for a lawsuit.

I recently stumbled across a highly instructive website, maintained by Columbia University, at KeepYourCopyright.org. It includes this entertaining and instructive feature that gathers together 173 different clauses from contracts with writers and other creative people, and rates each clause as "creator-friendly," "could be worse," "creator-unfriendly," or "incredibly overreaching." Even more helpfully, the site explains in a paragraph or two the reasons for each rating. You may find it useful to compare the key clauses posted on this site with the corresponding clauses in any contract you are offered. It can be illuminating.

http://www.keepyourcopyrights.org/

The Science Fiction Writers Association has a good introduction to publishing contracts on its website, as well as a few specimen agreements.

http://www.sfwa.org/category/information-center/contracts-and-copyrights/sample-contracts/

Many publishing lawyers own a copy of *Perle & Williams on Publishing Law;* pertinent portions relating to publishing contracts may now be viewed through Google Books. Non-lawyers will actually find it quite readable. Similarly, a useful chapter from Roy

Kaufman's *Drafting Print and Online Agreements* may also be accessed through Google Books. I frequently consult Roy's fine collection of model agreements in my publishing business.

There is an attorney that I have followed for years that is really very good. Lloyd J. Jassin is a book publishing and entertainment attorney. His practice includes drafting and negotiating publishing and entertainment industry contracts, copyright counseling, manuscript (libel) vetting, trademark registration, prosecution and litigation. Before law school, Lloyd was Director of Publicity of Prentice Hall Press. He is the coauthor of "The Copyright Permission and Libel Handbook" (John Wiley & Sons), counsel to the Publishers Marketing Association (PMA), and Vice Chair of the Small Press Center.

Contact: 212-354-4442; Jassin@copylaw.com or visit www.copylaw.com.

He publishes a checklist that I use personally. Here it is and it can be found online here: http://www.copylaw.com/new_articles/final.three.html

Book Contract Checklist

I. **General Provisions**
    1. Name/address of parties
    2. Description of work (synopsis)
    -Tentative title, no. of words, illus, intended audience, fiction, non-fiction, etc.

II. **Grant of Rights and Territory**
    1. Is it an assignment of "all rights" or a license agreement?
    2. Term or time period (i.e., usually the life of the copyright)
    3. Geographic scope
        a)   The world?
        b)   Limited (e.g., U.S., its possessions and Canada)
    4. Exclusive rights granted
        a)   Primary rights
          -Hardcover

-Trade paperback
-Mass market
-Direct mail
b)   Secondary (subsidiary rights)
-Periodical rights
1) First serial (i.e., pre-publication excerpts)
2) Second serial
-Book club
-Dramatic rights
-Film/TV rights
-Videocassette/audiocassette
-Radio rights
-Merchandising (commercial tie-in) rights
-New technologies
-Foreign translations rights
-British Commonwealth rights

II. **Manuscript Delivery**
1. Delivery requirements
    a) When due? Is the date realistic? Time is of the essence?
    b) What format? Specify size of paper, spacing, margins, etc.
    c) What to deliver?
        -Number of manuscript copies, disks (what WP format?)
        -Index (who pays?)
        -Number of illustrations, charts, photos (who pays?)
    d) Copyright permissions and releases
        -Scope of rights (does it parallel grant of rights?)
        -Who pays?

2. Manuscript Acceptance
    a) Criteria: Satisfactory in "form and content" or at "sole discretion" of the
        publisher? (note: acceptability is a often "flashpoint" for litigation)
    b) Termination for unsatisfactory manuscript
    c) Termination for changed market conditions
    d) How is notice of acceptance or dissatisfaction given
    e) Good faith duty to edit
    f) Return of the author advance

11

-*First proceeds* clause
-*False first proceeds* clause

III. **Copyright Ownership**
1. In whose name will work be registered?
2. When will work be registered? (Should be done within statutory period)
3. Joint authors and collaboration agreements
4. Work for hire
5. Reserved rights

IV. **Author's Representations & Warranties**
1. Author sole creator
2. Not previously published; not in public domain
3. Does not infringe any copyrights
4. Does not invade right of privacy or publicity
5. Not libelous or obscene
6. No errors or omissions in any recipe, formula or instructions
7. Limited only to material delivered by Author

V. **Indemnity & Insurance Provisions**
1. Author indemnifies publisher
2. Does indemnity apply to *claims* and *breaches*?
3. Can publisher withhold legal expenses? Is it held in interest bearing   account?
4. Is author added as additional insured on publisher's insurance?
5. Does publisher have ability to settle claims without prior approval of
author? If so, is there a dollar amount limitation?

VI. **Publication**
1. Duty to Publish within [insert number] months
   a) Force majeure (acts of god)
      - Any cap on delays?
2. Advertising and promotion
3. Right to use author's approved name and likeness
4. Bound galleys/review copies
5. Style or manner of publication
   a) Title consultation or approval?

b) Book jacket
- Right of consultation? Approval?
c) Changes in manuscript
6. Initial publication by specific imprint or publisher may sublicense rights?

V. **Money Issues**
1. Advance against future royalties
2. When payable? (in halves, thirds, etc.)
3. Royalties and subsidiary rights:
a) Primary rights
-Hardcover royalties
-Trade paperback royalties
-Mass market royalties
-Ebook royalties
-Royalty escalation(s)
-Bestseller bonus
-Royalty reductions
1) deep discount and special sales
2) mail order sales
3) premium sales
4) small printing
5) slow moving inventory

b) Secondary (subsidiary) rights royalty splits
-Book club (sales from publisher's inventory v. licensing rights)
-Serialization (first serial, second serial)
-Anthologies, selection rights
-Large print editions
-Hardcover
-Trade paperback
-Mass market
-Foreign translation
-British Commonwealth
-Future (i.e., new) technology rights
Is the right to intermingle with third party content included?
-Audio rights

-Motion picture/TV
-Merchandising

4. Reasonable reserve for returns
   a) What percentage withheld?
   b) When liquidated?

5. What is royalty based on? (retail price? wholesale price? net price?)
   a) At average discount of 50%, 20% of *net* is same as 10% of list
   b) At average discount of 40%, 16-2/3% of *net* is same as 10% of list
   c) At average discount of 20%, 12-1/2% of *net* is the same as 10% of list
6. Recoupment of advances

VI. **Accounting Statements**
1. Annual, semiannual, or quarterly statements
2. Payment dates
3. Cross-collateralization
4. Audit rights
5. Limit on time to object to statements
6. Limit on time to bring legal action
7. Examination on contingency basis
8. Pass through clause for subsidiary rights income
9. Reversion of rights for failure to account (important clause with smaller houses)

VII. **Revised Editions**
1. Frequency
2. By whom?
3. Royalty reductions if done by third party
4. Sale of revised edition treated as sale of new book?
5. Reviser/Author credit

VIII. **Option**
1. Definition of *next work*
2. When does option period start?

3. Definiteness of terms (i.e., is option legally enforceable?)
4. What type of option? (e.g., first look, matching, topping)

IX. **Competing Works**
1. How is *competing work* defined?
2. How long does non-compete run?
3. Any reasonable accommodations?

X. **Out-of-Print**
1. How defined?
2. Notice requirements
3. Author's right to purchase plates, film, inventory

XI. **Termination**
1. What triggers reversion of rights?
    a) Failure to publish within [insert number] months of manuscript acceptance
    b) Failure to account to author after due notice
    c) Failure to keep book in print (see Section X)
2. Survival of Author's representations and warranties
3. Licenses granted prior to termination survive

XII. **Miscellaneous**
1. Choice of governing law
2. Mediation / Arbitration clauses
3. Bankruptcy
4. Modification
5. Literary agency clause

Okay, let's move on and discuss the Anatomy of a Publishing Agreement by pulling apart the one I use all the time (it is in the download portal).

Chapter 2 – The Anatomy of a Publishing Agreement

Publishing Contract

ublishers exclusive world-wide electronic and print
l for all renewals and extensions of copyright. This

gital formats including all online formats carried
Plxmac.com 84596254

In this chapter, I want to pull apart a publishing agreement and point what is essential and what is pure boilerplate. Here is the agreement I use most often personally: My comments are in *italics…*

PUBLISHING AGREEMENT

This AGREEMENT is being made on Date, by and between Author's Name, with a mailing address of Author's Mailing Address ("the Author") and Publisher's Name, with a mailing address of Publisher's Mailing Address ("the Publisher") with reference to a work tentatively titled. *This is important: Under the Author's name clause I never use my personal name but have my children's trusts own all of my books. You can use your personal name such as "Dr. Leland Benton and/or assignees" and then assign it to family trusts or some type of owning entity for tax purposes. Consult a tax attorney on this one (not a CPA).*

"Tentative Title" (hereinafter "the Work"), which is described as follows:

Work Description.

Be as descriptive as possible in the work description.

WHEREBY, in consideration of the promises set forth in this Agreement, the Author and the Publisher agree as follows:

1) GRANT OF RIGHTS

The Author grants to the Publisher an exclusive right to publish, reproduce and distribute the Work in all formats described in Paragraph 5 below and ancillary paper products in non-book formats referred to in Paragraph 5 (a) (10) in all languages, and to exercise and grant to third parties the rights to the Work described in Paragraph 6 throughout the world ("the Territory") for the full term of the copyright under the present and future laws of any country in the Territory. Subject to the terms and conditions of this Agreement, the Author also grants to the Publisher the sole and exclusive right to advertise and promote the Work, including, but not limited to, the right to print, publish, license and/or sell excerpts and/or portions of the Work; provided, however, that Author shall have the right to participate in further promotion, advertising and marketing efforts with the good faith intent of increasing sales and distribution of the Work. <u>Notwithstanding anything in the foregoing, the grant of rights described herein in no way constitutes a transfer of the Author's right, title or interest in the copyright to the Work or in the paper rights to the individual images that each belong to the Author and which collectively constitute the Work, which is retained exclusively by Author at all times</u>

NOTE: I have underlined the essential clause above that must always be in the agreement to protect the author's ownership and copyright.

2) MANUSCRIPT DELIVERY

a) Timely delivery of complete materials for the Work is an essential condition of this Agreement insofar as the Publisher is concerned and is an essential consideration for Publisher's obligations hereunder. Accordingly, the parties hereby agree as follows:

(i) The Author shall deliver to the Publisher by Date of Delivery (a) the complete manuscript for the Work, approximately #Words words in length, acceptable to the Publisher, as a print-out on 8 1/2" x 11" paper and in digital format; and (b) all photographs, drawings, pictures and visual material necessary to the Work (collectively "artwork") in camera-ready form. The Author is responsible for supplying the art in form and content specified by the Publisher, which is to be determined on a case-by-case basis, either in camera-ready form or as digital files *(this is negotiable)*. The art must be supplied in an organized fashion and clearly labeled for the editor and designer.

(ii) The Author shall, at the Author's expense *(this is negotiable)*, obtain and deliver to the Publisher, with the complete manuscript all written permissions required by the Publisher for any text or artwork from other sources, and/or text and artwork whose rights do not belong to the Author, to be included in the Work by the Author.

(iii) If the Author fails to deliver the manuscript and/or artwork and permissions required by the foregoing clauses (i) and (ii) by the date set forth in clause (i), the Publisher shall have the right, in its sole discretion: *(the following are standard penalty clauses and all of it are negotiable. As you can see the penalties can be stiff so do not violate this clause)*

(A) To send written notice to the Author terminating any further obligations of the Publisher hereunder, upon receipt of which (I) the Author shall reimburse to the Publisher an amount equal to the advance against royalties paid to date pursuant to this Agreement and production fee, if any, paid by the Publisher; provided that Author shall not be obligated in any way to pay an amount greater than the total amount of the advance paid as of the date of termination (II) all rights (including pursuant to the grant of any license to use copyrighted materials, publication, and licensing rights) previously granted to Publisher hereunder shall automatically revert back to the Author, and (III) this Agreement shall be void and of no further force and effect; or

(B) To send written notice to the Author agreeing to a new delivery date, without limiting the Publisher's rights pursuant to clause (A) above should the Author not meet the new delivery date;

(iv) If the complete manuscript and/or artwork delivered by the Author is not acceptable to the Publisher in its sole, good faith editorial or business judgment, the Publisher shall have the right, in its sole discretion:

(A) To send written notice to the Author terminating any further obligations of the Publisher hereunder, in which event the Author shall have the right to license rights of any kind in and to the Work to a third party, subject to the condition and obligation to repay to the Publisher an amount equal to the advance against royalties and production fee, if any, paid by the Publisher pursuant to this Agreement, it being understood that the Publisher's exclusive rights hereunder shall continue in effect until such repayment of the advance to the Publisher has been made in full; or

(B) To give the Author a request for changes and revisions, in which event the Author shall have 30 days from the Author's receipt of such a request to deliver to the Publisher a revised manuscript of the Work that is acceptable to the Publisher in its sole discretion. If the Publisher proceeds under this clause (B) and the Author fails to deliver a revised manuscript within such 30 day period, Paragraph 2(a)(iii) shall apply, and if the Author delivers a revised manuscript which is not acceptable to the Publisher in its sole editorial or business judgment, this Paragraph 2(a)(iv) shall again apply.

b) Publisher shall advise the Author of its acceptance of the complete Work by written notice to the Author signed by an authorized officer of the Publisher. Comments, requests for revisions, or other communications to the Author from the Publisher shall not be deemed notice of acceptance or rejection by the Publisher. Payment of an installment of an advance shall not constitute notice of acceptance, unless the Publisher expressly notifies the Author in writing that such payment is intended as notice of acceptance.

c) The Work shall be the Author's next published book and the Author shall not offer rights to another book to another publisher nor accept an offer for another book from another publisher until a complete manuscript for the Work has been delivered to and accepted by the Publisher and the Author has complied with the option provisions of Paragraph 12. This provision shall apply to books co-authored by the Author as well as books written solely by the Author.

d) Should original text or original artwork or stock artwork not provided by the Author be required for the Work, the Publisher shall select a writer or an artist, as the case may be, whose work is consistent with the image of the Work, and that is reasonably acceptable to Author to prepare such text and/or artwork. Unless otherwise agreed, the cost thereof shall be paid by the Publisher, and the fee for such text and/or artwork shall be reimbursed to Publisher through future royalties as provided herein.

e) If the Publisher has sold a foreign co-edition or a book club edition of the Work, then the Author's delivery and review deadlines, as determined by the original schedule, become imperative, and if the Author fails to meet his/her deadline requirements, except for reasons beyond her reasonable control, and solely to the extent such delay is the direct result of the willful delay by Author, the Publisher is penalized by such a delay with loss of sale, more than 15% of extra manufacturing costs above the original estimated costs, or other additional expenses actually incurred as a direct result of such delay, the Publisher may deduct such losses from the Author's future royalties.

3) **EDITING AND PROOFS**

a) After the text and/or artwork have been accepted by the Publisher, no changes that significantly alter the concept of the Work may be made without the Author's approval. However, the Publisher may copyedit the Work in accordance with its standards of punctuation, spelling, capitalization, and usage. The Publisher shall send the copyedited manuscript to the Author, who shall make any revisions and corrections and return it within the time reasonably requested by the Publisher, not to exceed two weeks after receipt, or such other time frame agreed to by the parties. *(On the surface, this clause may seem no "big thing" but it is because an author does not want his Work co-opted by a publisher and any changes need to be approved by the author. You would be surprised as to the amount of litigation that has arisen because of publishers changing an author's Work.)*

b)   The Author shall review and return within the time reasonably requested by the Publisher, not to exceed two weeks from receipt (or other mutually agreed upon time period) proofs or other production materials submitted by the Publisher. The Author shall pay all charges in excess of 10% of the cost of filmwork *(this is negotiable)* of the Work for changes (other than corrections of printer's errors or changes made at the Publisher's request) that the Author makes to the Work after type has been set in conformity with the copyedited manuscript and for all changes in second or subsequent printings requested by the Author or necessitated in the Publisher's sole discretion as a result of third party claims. These costs shall be charged to the Author's/royalty accounts, except the Author shall upon request pay directly such charges that are in excess of 15% of the original cost of filmwork of the Work *(ALL NEGOTIABLE).*

4)   **PUBLICATION**

a)   The Publisher shall publish editions(s) of the Work in such format, style, and manner as the Publisher deems appropriate within 18 months from the date *(VERY IMPORTANT: Always articulate the exact time your Work will be published)* of the Publisher's acceptance of the manuscript and/or artwork for the Work, provided the Author has complied with Paragraphs 2(a) (ii) and 3 and has responded in a satisfactory way to any requests made under Paragraph 9(d). All details of publication, including but not limited to manufacture, format and design, cover treatment, distribution, pricing, advertising and promotion and distribution of free copies, shall be determined by the Publisher <u>in its sole discretion</u> *(NO FLIPPING WAY AT ITS SOLE DISCRETION. THIS NEEDS TO BE NEGOITATED OUT OF THE CONTRACT)* following consultation and discussions with the Author, and reasonably considering in good faith Author's opinion on such matters. Notwithstanding the foregoing, Publisher agrees that in any event, Author shall be given credit as the author and editor of the Work, and shall clearly indicate the same in writing in the final published Work. In the event of delay due to causes beyond the control of the Publisher, publication may be postponed until the next spring or fall season immediately succeeding the removal of the cause of the delay. In the event of such delay, Author shall not incur or be liable for any charges, fees, or costs. *(I ALWAYS INSERT A PENALTY CLAUSE AGAINST THE PUBLISHERS FOR ANY DELAYS WHETHER THE DELAY IS THEIR FAULT OR NOT)*

b) The Publisher shall give the Author 25 copies *(THIS IS NEGOTIABLE)*of each of the Publisher's editions of the Work on publication of the first edition of the book, and one copy each of any subsequent, co-edition, or licensed edition. The Author may purchase additional copies for personal use at a discount of 50% off the U.S. retail price; such purchases shall not be used for resale. The Author is responsible for the cost of shipping any additional copies Author purchases. *(I NEVER PAY FOR COPIES…NEVER!)*

5) ROYALTIES AND PAYMENT OF ADVANCE

a) The Publisher shall pay to the Author royalties on sales of finished copies of the Publisher's editions of the Work, less returns, and a reasonable allowance for returns, as follows:

(1) On all hardcover copies sold through ordinary channels of trade (except as otherwise provided below), 7.5% of the net amounts received by Publisher. "Net amounts received" shall mean the amount invoiced to customers based on the U.S. retail price, after discounts and exclusive of freight or special services on all copies sold. *(ALL NEGOTIABLE)*

(2) On all hardcover copies sold (i) on a non-returnable basis: or (ii) as special sales, as premiums, to catalog accounts, to book clubs, to book fairs or outside the ordinary channels of the book trade, 5% of the net amounts received by the Publisher; *(ALL NEGOTIABLE)*

(3) On all hardcover copies sold outside the United States or for export to other countries throughout the Territory, 5% of the net amounts received by the Publisher; *(ALL NEGOTIABLE)*

(4) On all paperback copies sold through ordinary channels of trade (except as otherwise provided below), 5% of the net amounts received by Publisher. *(ALL NEGOTIABLE)*

(5) On all paperback copies sold at discounts higher than the Publisher's announced discounts for wholesale and retail accounts in the book trade and (i) on a non-returnable basis; or (ii) as special sales, as premiums, to catalog accounts, to book fairs or outside of the ordinary channels of the book trade, 5% of the net amounts received by the Publisher; *(ALL NEGOTIABLE)*

(6) On all copies of the Publisher's editions of the Work sold directly by the Publisher to consumers in response to mail order or other direct-response solicitations sponsored by the Publisher, 2.5% of the net amount received by Publisher, exclusive of shipping, handling, and taxes; *(ALL NEGOTIABLE)*

(7) On copies sold from a reprinting of 1,500 copies or less or where the mark up (Retail price divided by actual manufacturing cost) is less than 5 times made one year or more after the first publication of the Work: one-half of the prevailing royalty rate then in effect. *(ALL NEGOTIABLE)*

(8) On all copies of the Publisher's editions of the Work sold as remainders at more than the cost of manufacture, 5% of the net amount received by the Publisher; (The Publisher shall use its best efforts to give the Author notice of the Publisher's intention to remainder copies of the Work; the Publisher shall offer the Author copies of the Work, and give the Author a reasonable opportunity to purchase additional copies at the Publisher's remainder price;

however, the Publisher's failure to do so shall not be considered a breach of this Agreement nor give the Author any claim for damages); *(ALL NEGOTIABLE)*

(9) On copies given to or sold to the Author, given away to promote sales or to charitable institutions, sold at or below the cost of manufacture or damaged, stolen or destroyed, no royalties shall be paid; *(ALL NEGOTIABLE)*

(10) On ancillary paper products; that is paper products derivative of the Work, such as boxed notecards, wall calendars, desk diaries, and the like, 3% of the net amounts received by the Publisher.

b)   Only copies sold under Paragraphs 5(a) (1) and 5(a) (4) shall be counted in determining royalty escalations, if any. *(ALL NEGOTIABLE)*

c)   As an advance against all royalties and all proceeds from the disposition of subsidiary rights due to the Author under this Agreement, the Publisher shall pay to the Author the sum of $10,000 payable in full, thirty (30) days from date of signature of this Agreement and completion of accompanying Author Questionnaire. *(ALL NEGOTIABLE)*

The parties hereto agree and acknowledge that the Publisher shall have the right to withhold and retain all royalties and other monies payable to the Author hereunder until it shall have recouped the full amount of the advance paid to the Author. *(ALL NEGOTIABLE)*

6)   **SUBSIDIARY RIGHTS**

The Author grants and assigns to the Publisher the right, solely and exclusively (except as otherwise indicated), to dispose of or to license the disposition of the subsidiary rights described below in and to the Work, and the net profits received by the Publisher from any such disposition to a third party after the Publisher recoups from the gross proceeds the Publisher's direct out-of-pocket expenses related to the actual sale of such rights shall be divided between the Author and the Publisher as specified: *(ALL NEGOTIABLE)*

		Author's Percentage	Publisher's Percentage
(1)	periodical or newspaper publication prior to book publication (hereinafter "first serial");	50	50
(2)	periodical or newspaper publication following book publication, including syndication rights;	50	50
(3)	permissions, including condensation, abridgment, digest, selections, anthologies, textbook, or book fair editions;	50	50
(4)	special hardcover reprint editions;	50	50
(5)	the non-exclusive right to record and transmit and display the Work, or part of the Work, by any means, electronic or otherwise, including the right to include the Work or quotations from the Work in information storage and retrieval systems, databases, computer software, audio and video cassette and in multimedia products adapted from the Work. In no event shall the foregoing be interpreted as a grant to the Publisher of dramatic film adaptation rights, or as any exclusive grant to display the Work or portions thereof in a photographic or other art gallery, which rights are retained by Author in all respects;	50	50

(ALL OF THE ABOVE SCHEDULE IS NEGOTIABLE)

(6)   The Author further grants to the Publisher the right to arrange for editions of the Work to be published by book clubs, in foreign languages and/or by foreign publishers (including the right to sub-license to foreign language publishers or to foreign publishers the

other rights granted in this Agreement) and special paperback reprint editions. "Foreign publishers" are publishers located outside the United States and Canada.

(7)　In the event that the Publisher licenses the publication of foreign language or book club editions of the Work, the Publisher shall pay the Author 10% of the gross licensing fee received. In the event that the Publisher manufactures editions of the Work for publication in foreign countries and/or foreign languages or by book clubs, the Publisher shall pay the Author 10% of the amount received by the Publisher net of prepress and production expenses for such editions of the Work. *(ALL NEGOTIABLE)*

7)　**ACCOUNTING**

(PAY VERY CLOSE ATTENTION TO THIS SECTION)

a)　Following first publication of the Work by the Publisher, an accounting of all of the Author's earnings under the terms of this Agreement, accompanied by payment of amounts due on such accounting, shall be rendered no later than May 31 of each year for the period ending the preceding December 31; provided that the Publisher need not send accountings if the amounts due to the Author are less than $100, unless requested in writing by the Author, which request may be given not more than once during each 12 month period. *(ALL NEGOTIABLE)*

b)　The Publisher may retain on any accounting statements a reserve against returns, which the Publisher in its sole discretion deems reasonable, provided the amount of the reserve held is clearly indicated and provided the subsequent statements clearly indicated how such a reserve has been applied. On request, the Publisher shall provide a written explanation of any reserve. *(ALL NEGOTIABLE)*

c)　If the Author receives an overpayment of royalties because of copies reported sold but subsequently returned, the Publisher may deduct the amount of the overpayment from the further sums due the Author under this Agreement. *(ALL NEGOTIABLE)*

d) Any sums owed by the Author to the Publisher under this Agreement may be deducted from any sums due the Author by the Publisher under this Agreement. *(ALL NEGOTIABLE AS TO THE AMOUNTS AND TIME OF DEDUCTION)*

8) RIGHT TO AUDIT

(PAY VERY CLOSE ATTENTION TO THIS SECTION TOO)

a) Upon written request from the Author sent not more than twice in any 12-month period, the Publisher shall provide the following information: the number of copies of each edition of the Work printed by the Publisher, the date of each printing; the cumulative number of copies sold, returned, distributed free of charge, remaindered, destroyed or lost; copies of any licenses made by the Publisher; and any other information the Author may reasonably request on the basis that it is required in order to ascertain the accuracy of accountings rendered.

b) The Author may upon written notice and through accountants experienced in the US book publishing business examine the Publisher's records relating to the Work during normal business hours under such conditions as the Publisher may reasonably prescribe. An audit with respect to any accounting statement shall not begin later than 12 months from the date said statement was sent to Author, nor shall any audit continue for longer than 5 consecutive business days, nor shall audits be made more frequently than twice annually nor shall the time period or the records supporting any such statements be audited more than once. If an error is discovered as a result of any such examination, the party in whose favor the error was made shall promptly pay the other the amount of the error. Any such examination shall be at the Author's expense unless errors of accounting in the Publisher's favor amounting to 5% or more of the total sum paid to the Author under the statement(s) being audited are found, in which event the Publisher shall reimburse Author for the cost of the examination up to the amount of the underpayment found as well as repay the underpayment. *(ALL NEGOTIABLE)*

c) Accountings from the Publisher shall be deemed final and binding between Author and Publisher on the date two years from the date such accounting was rendered by the Publisher unless such accounting has been disputed in writing prior to such date, setting forth the specific objections to such accounting and the details supporting such objections. *(ALL NEGOTIABLE)*

9) **WARRANTIES AND INDEMNITIES**

(THIS IS A VERY IMPORTANT PART OF A PUBLISHING AGREEMENT TO PROTECT THE PUBLISHER. MAKE SURE THAT EVERYTHING YOU WARRANT HERE IS TRUE.)

a)   The Author warrants to the Publisher that:

(i)   At the time of publication of the Work, the Author will be the sole author of the Work and rights granted in this Agreement and shall have secured those rights according to Paragraph 2(a) (ii),

(ii)   As of the date hereof, Author has not assigned, pledged, or otherwise encumbered them and has the right to enter into this Agreement and to perform Author's obligations hereunder;

(ii) As of the date hereof, to the best of Author's knowledge based on his/her due diligence, the Work is an original work* (except to the extent that it includes previously published material for which Author has in her possession or is in the process of obtaining any necessary written permission which may be delivered to Publisher, if requested), is free of any lien, claim, or debt of any kind, is not in the public domain in any country in the Territory and that the Work is protected by to the best of Author's knowledge, and will continue to be protected by in the countries in which and during the term the Publisher has rights hereunder; and

(iii) The Work contains no material that is libelous, obscene, plagiarized or any other unlawful matter, or is in any way illegal, and that upon obtaining the permissions of use referred to herein above, it in no way infringes upon the copyright or violates any other right of any person so as to subject the Publisher to liability to any third party.

b) The Author shall indemnify the Publisher, its distributors, employees, licensees, agents and any retailer from any loss, damage, expense (including reasonable attorneys' fees and expenses), recovery or judgment arising from any breach or alleged breach of any of the Author's warranties, subject to the limitations stated below.

(i) Each party shall promptly inform the other of any claim made against either which, if sustained, would constitute a breach of any warranty made by the Author to the Publisher in this Agreement. The Publisher shall defend any such claim made against the Publisher with counsel of the Publisher's selection. The Author shall fully cooperate with the Publisher in such defense and may join in such defense with counsel of the Author's selection at the Author's expense.

(ii) If the Publisher wishes to settle on its own behalf any claim made against the Publisher, the Publisher shall consult with the Author and give serious consideration to any objections the Author may have, and the Author and the Publisher shall attempt in good faith to agree in writing on the percentage of any such settlement costs and defense costs which each shall bear. Failing such agreement, the Publisher may on its own behalf settle any such claim made against the Publisher on terms the Publisher deems advisable. In such event, the Publisher may recover from the Author amounts paid in settlement and defense costs if such costs are incurred because of a breach of warranty made by the Author to the Publisher in this Agreement. Alternatively, the Author may, at the Author's discretion, provide security reasonably acceptable to the Publisher for the further costs of defending the claim, in which event the Publisher shall not settle without the Author's written consent. *(NO FLIPPING WAY. PUBLISHER MUST ALWAYS SEEK AND SECURE APPROVAL FROM AUTHOR AS TO ANY SETTLEMENT UNLESS AUTHOR IS HELD HARMLESS FOR ANY PENALTIES, WHICH IS WHAT I PUT IN MY AGREEMENTS)*

c) The Author shall be responsible for any claims made against any third party to which the Publisher grants subsidiary rights to the Work to the same extent as the Author is responsible to the Publisher under the indemnification provisions of this Agreement. The warranties and indemnities made by the Author in this Agreement shall survive the termination of this Agreement. *(THIS MUST BE APPROVED BY AUTHOR IN ADVANCE OF GRANTING ANY THIRD PARTY RIGHTS.)*

d) Prior to the first publication of the Work, the Publisher may have the Work read by the Publisher's counsel at the Publisher's expense. If the Author will not make changes recommended by the Publisher's counsel, the Publisher shall not be required to publish the Work and shall have the right to recover from the Author any advances made to the Author under this Agreement, plus interest thereon at a rate of 12% per annum or the maximum permitted by law, whichever is less, from the date the advance was paid by the Publisher through the date of repayment to the Publisher. When such advances are fully repaid, this Agreement shall terminate. NO FLIPPING WAY DOES THE PUBLISHER HAVE THE RIGHT TO RECOVER ADANCED FEES BECAUSE THE AUTHOR WILL NOT MAKE CHANGES TO HIS/HER WORK RECOMMENDED BY PUBLISHER'S COUNSEL.)

10) **RESERVED RIGHTS AND NON-COMPETITION**

a) During the term of this Agreement, the Author will not exercise or dispose of any reserved rights, nor cause to be published any version of the Work, or any similar work, in such a way as to intentionally affect in a materially adverse fashion the value of any of the rights granted to Publisher hereunder.

All rights to the Work not specifically granted to the Publisher in this Agreement are reserved by the Author. In exercising such rights, the Author shall reserve for the Publisher's benefit the rights granted to the Publisher in this Agreement and, in addition, shall comply with the following if the following rights have not been granted to the Publisher in this Agreement:

(i) In connection with the Author's disposition of reserved first serial rights, the Author shall consult with the Publisher about the timing of the first serial publication and shall not, without the written consent of the Publisher, permit the publication in newspapers or periodicals of more than 5% of the Work nor any condensation of the entire Work. The Author shall require any licensee of such rights to carry a credit to the publication of the Work by the Publisher; and/or

(ii) In connection with the Author's disposition of reserved motion picture, television, radio, live-stage dramatic adaptation or audio-visual adaptation rights, the Author shall not make any grant of publication rights without the Publisher's written consent (which consent shall not be unreasonably conditioned, withheld, or delayed) and shall in no event make any grant of novelization, photonovel, comic book, or similar rights. The Publisher will consent to the publication of synopses of motion pictures and television dramatic adaptations of the Work, provided each such synopsis is published with an appropriate copyright notice.

b)   During the term hereof, the Author shall not publish, or permit to be published, any book on the same or similar subject matter as the Work that would in the opinion of the Publisher, compete in the market place with sales of the Work or detract from sales of the Work.

11) **COPYRIGHT**

a)   Prior to publication of the Work, the Publisher shall print a copyright notice in conformity with the United States Copyright Act and the Universal Copyright Convention in the name of the Author in each copy of the Work printed by the Publisher, and shall require its licensees to do the same. The Publisher shall register the copyright on the Work with the United States Copyright Office within first year of publication. *(THIS IS IMPORTANT)*

b)   Any textual or illustrative material prepared for the Work by the Publisher or under separate contract to the Publisher at its expense may be copyrighted separately as the Publisher deems appropriate.

(NO! AUTHOR RETAINS OWNERSHIP OF ANY MATERIAL PREPARED BY PUBLISHER AND NOT THE PUBLISHER)

c)   All references to copyright in this Agreement shall reflect any amendment made subsequent to the date of this Agreement in the copyright laws of the United States, in any international copyright conventions or in the copyright laws of any other country within the Territory. Both parties shall execute such documents as the Publisher may request to effectuate copyright to the Work in accordance with this Agreement.

d)   In the event of any infringement of the copyright of the Work or of any of the exclusive rights granted to the Publisher hereunder, the Publisher may employ such remedies as it deems advisable and may name the Author a co-plaintiff in any litigation the Publisher may commence.   (IMPORTANT;   PUBLISHER   MUST   SEEK AUTHOR'S APPROVAL PRIOR TO BEING NAMED CO-PLAINTIFF)   The Publisher shall bear the entire expense of any such litigation. Any recovery shall be applied first to reimburse the Publisher for its expenses; the balance shall be divided between the Author and the Publisher as follows: that portion which is based on actual damages shall be divided in proportion to the losses from such infringement suffered by each, and that portion which is based upon the infringer's profits, statutory damages, or punitive damages shall be divided equally.

12)   **OPTION**

In further consideration of this Agreement, for a period up to 1 year following initial publication of the Work, the Author grants to the Publisher an option on the Author's next book-length work ("the option book"), such option to be exercised as follows. The Author shall submit to the Publisher a complete manuscript, including artwork for the option book before offering rights to the option book to any other party. The Publisher shall have 30 days from its receipt of the option book to advise the Author whether it wishes to publish the option book and upon what financial terms, such 30-day period to commence no earlier than 60 days following the Publisher's first publication of the Work. If within such a 30-day period the

Publisher does not advise the Author that it wishes to publish the option book, the Author may offer the option book to other parties without further obligation to the Publisher. If within such a 30-day period the Publisher does advise the Author that it wishes to publish the option book but within 30 days of the Publisher so advising the Author, the Author and the Publisher have not agreed on financial terms for such publication, the Author may offer the option book to other publishers; however, the Author shall, prior to the acceptance of an offer for the option book from any third party, submit the financial terms of such offer to the Publisher in writing and the Publisher shall have three business days to advise the Author whether it would publish the option book on such financial terms. If the Publisher does so, the Author will enter a contract with the Publisher incorporating all such financial terms and the other terms and conditions contained in this Agreement. This option provision shall apply to the next book co-authored by the Author as well as the next book solely authored by the Author.

13) AUTHOR'S RIGHTS OF TERMINATION

(THIS IS EXTREMELY IMPORTANT!!!!!)

a) If the Publisher does not publish the Work within the time specified in Paragraph 4(a) for reasons other than first serial or book club use, delays of the Author in returning the copyedited manuscript or proofs, the Author's failure to comply with requests made by the Publisher's counsel, or delays caused by circumstances beyond the Publisher's control, and if the Publisher at any time thereafter receives written notice from the Author demanding publication, the Publisher shall within 90 days of the Publisher's receipt of such written demand either publish the Work or revert to the Author in writing all rights to the Work granted to the Publisher in this Agreement, subject to any outstanding licenses, which shall be assigned to the Author, the Author shall retain any advance payments made under this Agreement prior to such reversion in full and complete satisfaction of the Publisher's obligations under this Agreement, and any and all rights granted to Publisher hereunder shall automatically revert to Author. *(I ALWAYS INCLUDE A*

PENALTY CLAUSE HERE AND NOT JUST KEEPING ANY ADVANCES.)

b)   (i) If the Work is out-of-print and the Publisher receives from the Author a written request for a reversion of rights, the Publisher shall within four months of the Publisher's receipt of such request do one of the following: (A) announce that it will reissue an edition of the Work under one of its imprints within one year from the date of such announcement; or (B) enter a license providing for the publication in the world of an edition of the Work within one year from the date of the license; or (C) revert in writing to the Author the rights granted to the Publisher in this Agreement. (If the Publisher does announce that it will reissue an edition of the Work but has not reissued an edition one year after such announcement, the rights shall on such date automatically revert to the Author.)

(ii) Any reversion shall be subject to grants of rights made to third parties prior to the date of the reversion and the right of the Author and the Publisher to participate in the proceeds from such grants on the terms hereof.

(iii) The Work shall be considered out-of-print if no edition as specified in Paragraph 1, above, Grant of Rights, is available for sale through ordinary channels of the book trade in North America from the order fulfillment department of the Publisher or from a licensee of the Publisher, and no license is in effect which provides for the distribution within one year from the date of the Author's request of an edition of the Work through ordinary channels of the book trade in North America.

14)   **FORCE MAJEURE**

The failure of the Publisher to publish or reissue the Work shall not be a breach of this Agreement or give rise to any right of termination or reversion if such failure is caused by restrictions of governmental agencies, labor disputes, inability to obtain materials necessary for manufacture of the Work, or any other reason beyond the Publisher's control; in the event of delay from any such cause, the publication or reissue shall be postponed for a period of time reasonably related to such cause.

15) **GENERAL PROVISIONS**

(i) The Author shall keep at least one copy of the manuscript of the Work and any other materials submitted to the Publisher under this Agreement. The Publisher shall not be responsible for the loss of or damage to any manuscript, artwork or other materials submitted by the Author.

(ii) No advertisements (other than advertisements for other publications of the Publisher) shall be included in any edition of the Work published by the Publisher or under the license from the Publisher without the Author's written consent.

(iii) The Publisher may use the Author's name, likeness, and biographical data reviewed and <u>approved of by Author</u> on any editions of the Work published by the Publisher and in any advertising, publicity, or promotion for the Work in any medium and may extend these rights in connection with grants of the subsidiary rights made by the Publisher.

(iv) The Author agrees to cooperate, and to be available, in connection with Publisher's requirements regarding the promotion, publicity, and advertising of the Work, including without limitation being available on a priority basis to make appearances and/or to grant interviews in connection with publication of the Work.

(v) If the Publisher is required by law to pay to any U.S. or foreign government taxing authority any portion of amounts due the Author under this Agreement, such payments shall be deducted from the amounts due the Author hereunder.

(vi) If any foreign taxes, bank charges, agents' commissions, transaction costs or collection costs are incurred or imposed in connection with any payments due the Publisher from the exercise of any right granted in this Agreement, the appropriate allocation of proceeds between the Publisher and the Author from the exercise of such rights shall be made on amounts received after such charges have been paid. *(ALWAYS REQUIRE A WRITTEN ACCOUNTING OF ANY FEES UNDER THIS CLAUSE)*

(vii) This Agreement shall be binding upon and inure to the benefit of Author and upon the successors or assigns of Publisher, but no assignment shall be binding on either party without the written consent of the other. For purposes of this Agreement, reference to Publisher shall include any assignee, parent, affiliate, subsidiary, or successor of Publisher by reason of merger, consolidation, sale or exchange of assets of Publisher or reorganization. No such merger, consolidation, sale or exchange of assets of Publisher or other reorganization shall be deemed breach of the provisions of this paragraph prohibiting assignment nor shall any assignment to a related corporate company. The Author shall have the right to assign any amounts due hereunder to the extent such amounts become due after the Publisher has received written notice from the Author of such assignment.

(viii) If, under any provision of this Agreement, the Publisher is required to obtain the Author's approval, such approval shall not be unreasonably withheld or delayed. If the Publisher fails to receive a response from the Author within such time from the Author's receipt of a request for approval as the Publisher may reasonably designate to accommodate its schedule for publication, promotion, or the exercise of rights when any approval is requested, the approval requested shall be deemed granted. *(NEVER WITHOLD APPROVAL OR DENY APPROVAL WITHIN THE TIME LIMITS OF THE AGREEMENT)*

(ix) This Agreement contains the entire understanding of the Author and the Publisher with reference to the Work; there are no warranties other than those expressly stated in this Agreement. No waiver or modification of any provision of this Agreement shall be valid unless in writing and signed by both parties. No waiver of any breach shall be deemed a waiver of any subsequent breach, or of a breach of any other provision of this Agreement. If any provision of this Agreement is held to be invalid or unenforceable, the remaining provisions shall not be affected.

(x) Regardless of its place of physical execution or performance, the provisions of this Agreement shall in all respects be construed according to, and the rights and liabilities to the parties hereto shall in all respects be governed by the laws of the State of State of Governing Law applicable to agreements entirely made and performed therein.

(xi) The caption headings of this Agreement are inserted for convenience only and are without substantive effect.

(xii) This Agreement shall be of no force and effect unless signed by both parties within 60 days of the date first stated above.

(xiii) All notices to be given hereunder shall be in writing sent by hand, or by overnight delivery, or by certified or registered mail and sent to the parties at their addresses first set forth above, or to such other address as either party may hereafter specify by written notice. Notices sent by hand or by overnight delivery service shall be deemed delivered when received; if sent by certified or registered mail, such notices shall be deemed delivered when received, or if rejected as of the date five days after the date on which sent.

(xiv) The state or federal courts in the County of County of Jurisdiction (and courts with appellate jurisdiction therefrom) shall have exclusive jurisdiction of all disputes concerning or relating to this Agreement, its interpretation, performance by the parties and/or any breach thereof, and venue in such courts is proper and convenient.

16) **AGENCY**

The Author confirms that the party named in the Addendum, if any (herein called the Agent), has acted as the Author's agent in connection with the negotiation of this Agreement. The Author hereby authorizes the Agent (a) to collect and receive all sums of money payable to the Author hereunder; and (b) to act in the Author's behalf in all matters arising out of this Agreement.

IN WITNESS WHEREOF, the parties have signed this Agreement to be effective as of the date first stated above.

AUTHOR

Author's Name

PUBLISHER

Publisher's Name

Author's Tax Identification Number:

Author's Birth Date:

(This information is needed for copyright purposes)

ADDENDUM TO AGREEMENT

1. a) Provisional title of the Work:

b) Approximate specifications of Work:

Manuscript length (approx.):

Page count (approx.): #pages

Illustrations, number and type (approx.):

Trim size (approx.): 8x10 inches

Format: Hard Cover

On Sale Date:

Chapter 3 – The Art of Negotiating a Publishing Agreement

Let's make a deal, shall we? And the best deal you will find is one that you negotiate with a publisher so I am going to teach you the art of negotiation.

The Art of Negotiation – prior to any negotiations, develop a plan of what you want and need and write them down. Use this as a guide in your negotiations. The other side always appreciates when you come prepared. If the opposing side is bigger than you then make your concerns public of what bothers you about them. Will they steal your ideas and develop their own product. Are they there just to wring information from you? Put it out on the table and listen to their response. Also have two or three "fall back" positions where you can compromise and still get what you want. Next, come up with a list of reasons why your proposal would be beneficial to the opposing party. This is how I put on the table the positive "common ground". Also make a list of all points to be avoided; this will help you keep your focus on what you want and need.

1. First things first! You always begin negotiating from points of agreement and not disagreement. You begin with a positive and not a negative.

2. Take your ego out of the way! Since all negotiations eventually get to the valuation of what you are offering, it is easy to become offended and this will lead to contention.

3. Frame all of your negotiations around mutual interests rather than your personal interest alone.

4. Be respectful, it's more likely the other side will reciprocate.

5. Be wise, not smart. Rather than looking for short-term gratification that bolsters the ego—like assuming a power posture or making a joke at another's expense—keep your eye on the ball.

6. Publishers will press the point that you are a new author with no track record. Always respectfully tell them that the publishing business is in business to take risk and you are a good risk.

7. Do not use "I" statements. Use "we" statements. It is not "I want this;" it is "we need this to succeed together".

8. Pay close attention to body language. Do not sit back in your chair; lean forward in your chair and engage in eye contact.

9. In any negotiation, the prevailing concept is that there will be one winner and one loser. The best situation is two winners where both sides walk away satisfied.

10. In your preparation always look for the other side's weakness. Publishing is a tough game and publishers need good authors whose books sell. What genre are you writing in? How successful has the publisher been in this genre?

11. Identify and outline your goals and objectives at the outset of negotiations in an opening statement and ask the opposing party to do the same.

12. Good faith and flexibility define negotiations. If either one is absent then you are wasting your time.

13. There are two distinct types of negotiations. First, there is the type whereby one or both sides know exactly what the other side wants before going to the negotiating table, and secondly the type whereby both sides have agreed on a general objective but the actual positions of each side are not known until the parties reach the table.

14. TRY TO ANTICIPATE OPPOSING VIEWS AND REACTIONS ON EACH POINT AND PREPARE TO REFUTE OR REBUT THOSE VIEWPOINTS.

15. PUT YOURSELF THROUGH A 'DEVILS ADVOCATE' EXERCISE, WHEREBY YOU TEST EACH ONE OF YOUR POINTS AND POSITIONS TO SEE IF THEY ARE FAIR AND REASONABLE TO BOTH SIDES.

16. THOROUGHLY RESEARCH YOUR OPPOSITION'S BACKGROUND, REPUTATION, HISTORY, PERFORMANCE RECORD ON PREVIOUS AGREEMENTS OR CONTRACTS, ETC.

17. IF THE NEGOTIATION IS WITH FOREIGN INDIVIDUALS OR COUNTRIES, ALWAYS TRY TO SEND YOUR NOTES, POSITION PAPERS, DRAFT AGREEMENTS, ETC., TO THEM IN BOTH ENGLISH AND THEIR OWN LANGUAGE. This is important if negotiating foreign rights.

18. TRY TO OBTAIN AND MAINTAIN THE INITIATIVE AT THE CONFERENCE TABLE. Always attempt to take the lead and control of the negotiations.

19. PREPARE MEMORANDA AFTER EACH NEGOTIATING SESSION OF EXACTLY WHAT TRANSPIRED AT THE SESSION. Stay organized! I have been in negotiations lasting weeks and I review my

memorandums constantly to stay fully briefed. Also, if I send another member of my staff to negotiate then these memorandums keep me briefed on what is transpiring so I can send instructions to my negotiator.

20. THE MOST IMPORTANT NOT TO DO IS DISCUSS OR REVEAL YOUR NEGOTIATING POINTS AND POSITIONS TO ANYONE OUTSIDE OF THOSE WHO ABSOLUTELY NEED TO KNOW THEM.

21. NEVER MAKE CONCESSIONS TO YOUR OPPOSITION WITHOUT GETTING SOMETHING IN RETURN. ALWAYS TIE YOUR CONCESSIONS TO SOMETHING YOU WANT.

22. DO NOT TRY TO INGRATIATE YOURSELF TO THE OTHER SIDE OR BECOME WELL LIKED AND POPULAR DURING THE NEGOTIATION. Be polite and respectful but not sickening.

23. NEVER ARGUE OR DISAGREE AMONG YOURSELVES AT THE TABLE.

24. NEVER BLUFF ON A POINT UNLESS YOU ARE PREPARED TO HAVE YOUR BLUFF CALLED.

25. If the opposing party does not exercise good faith in the negotiations then reach across the table and smack the living snot out of him/her. Okay I made this one up just to see if you were paying attention.

Be sure to practice your body language in front of a mirror or camera. Body language is important. I wrote two books on the subject to assist you:

Body Language - Communication - Body Language is quite real and has become a pseudo-science. It is used in body language dating, and all personal and business relationships. Communication - Body Language is all about how to read other's thoughts and their gestures, communication skills, a body language training course, learning body language correctly, and learning the power of body language. A person uses more than words to communicate and body language can be a more effective communication medium than words. This book teaches how to identify and interpret all types of body language. Every professional person should understand and recognize the different forms of body language. You will use what you learn in Body Language in everyday life more so than anything else you have ever learned.

http://www.amazon.com/dp/B006INI18G

Body Talk - Non-Verbal Communication - Body Talk is NOT body language! Body Language is defined as an involuntary form of mental and physical ability of human non-verbal communication, which consists of body posture, gestures, facial expressions, and eye movements and purposeful body expression. Humans send and interpret such signals almost entirely subconsciously. Body Talk is defined as a voluntary and purposeful form of mental and physical ability of human non-verbal communication, which consists of body posture, gestures, facial expressions, and eye movements. Humans send and interpret such signals entirely consciously. Body Language is covert while Body Talk is overt. People practice Body Language without being knowingly aware they are doing it. People that use Body Talk are fully aware of what they are doing and in most cases are very good at it. Body Talk is used in business as well as personal. Business communication training teaches Body Talk. All Body Talk training and communication is an intense form of communication training. What is communication skill as it applies to Body Talk? It is a person's non-verbal skills. People use Body Talk all of the time. Think romance? That certain walk, the quick smile and eye contact. The skills of communication are very important in business and personal. Without Body Talk, a person cannot become successful!

http://www.amazon.com/dp/B0079MA1XS

Chapter 4 - Summary & Conclusions

Okay, allow me to sum everything up for you.

In Chapter 1 – The Need for Publishing Agreements, I provided you with valuable resources to check out especially as they pertain to your genre of writing.   Publishers do specialize in certain genres especially children's books, romance, and sci-fi genres.

Be sure to access and download the resources I have provided in the download portal.

In Chapter 2 – The Anatomy of a Publishing Agreement, I pulled apart a publishing agreement to demonstrate what was negotiable and what points you needed to consider carefully from an author's standpoint.

Be sure to read my comments that are in italics and commit to memory what they are. Formulate your own contract using the one I gave you in order to prepare for the actual negotiations.

In Chapter 3 – The Art of Negotiating a Publishing Agreement, my goal was to teach you the finer points of negotiating. I have been in literally thousands of negotiations and the points I outline represent years of experience. Remember, the best agreement is where both sides win.

I sincerely hope this book has helped you to better understand publishing agreements. They aren't scary or one-sided.   When negotiated correctly, they provide protection for both sides as well as to commit to writing exactly what is required of you as an author. Never violate any of the agreement's terms and conditions.

In choosing a publisher, it is important to remember that a reputable publisher NEVER asks for money upfront from an author and in fact, an author should never be required to front any kind of money whatsoever. Run away from any publisher requesting money upfront from an author.

So ends the lesson. I have a special gift for my readers so please read on...

I Have a Special Gift for My Readers

I appreciate my readers for without them I am just another author attempting to make a difference. If my book has made a favorable impression please leave me an honest review. Thank you in advance for you participation.

My readers and I have in common a passion for the written word as well as the desire to learn and grow from books.

My special offer to you is a massive ebook library that I have compiled over the years. It contains hundreds of fiction and non-fiction ebooks in Adobe Acrobat PDF format as well as the Greek classics and old literary classics too.

In fact, this library is so massive to completely download the entire library will require over 5 GBs open on your desktop.

Use the link below and scan all of the ebooks in the library. You can select the ebooks you want individually or download the entire library.

The link below does not expire after a given time period so you are free to return for more books rather than clog your desktop. And feel free to give the link to your friends who enjoy reading too.

I thank you for reading my book and hope if you are pleased that you will leave me an honest review so that I can improve my work and or write books that appeal to your interests.

Okay, here is the link…

http://tinyurl.com/special-readers-promo

PS: If you wish to reach me personally for any reason you may simply write to mailto:lee.benton@epubwealth.com.

I answer all of my emails so rest assured I will respond.

Meet the Author

Dr. Leland Benton is Director of Applied Web Info, a holding company for ePubWealth.com, a leading ePublisher company based in Utah. With over 21,000 resellers in over 22-countries, ePubWealth.com is a leader in ePublishing, book promotion, and ebook marketing.

As the creator and author of "The ePubWealth Program," Leland teaches up-and-coming authors the ins-and-outs of today's ePublishing world. He has assisted hundreds of authors make it big in the ePublishing world.

Leland also created a series of external book promotion programs and teaches authors how to promote their books using external marketing sources.

Leland is also the Managing Director of Applied Mind Sciences, the company's mind research unit and Chief Forensics Investigator for the company's ForensicsNation unit. He is active in privacy rights through the company's PrivacyNations unit and is an expert in survival planning and disaster relief through the company's SurvivalNations unit.

Leland resides in Southern Utah.

http://www.amazon.com/author/lelandbenton

Visit some of his websites
http://appliedmindsciences.com/
http://appliedwebinfo.com/
http://BoolbuilderPLUS.com
http://embarrassingproblemsfix.com/
http://www.epubwealth.com/
http://forensicsnation.com/
http://neternatives.com/
http://privacynations.com/

http://survivalnations.com/
http://thebentonkitchen.com
http://theolegions.org

Made in the USA
San Bernardino, CA
03 December 2016